Geography of the Americas

PACIFIC OCEAN

North America

United States

ATLANTIC OCEAN

Mexico   *Gulf of Mexico*

Central America

Caribbean Sea

South America

Rosie McCormick

Core Knowledge

ISBN: 978-1-68380-496-3

Geography of the Americas

Table of Contents

Using Maps

Maps come in all sizes and colors, and they show many different things. Some maps might show someone how to get to a park. Some maps show land features, such as mountains and valleys. Some maps show information about the weather. And others show a country—or even the whole world!

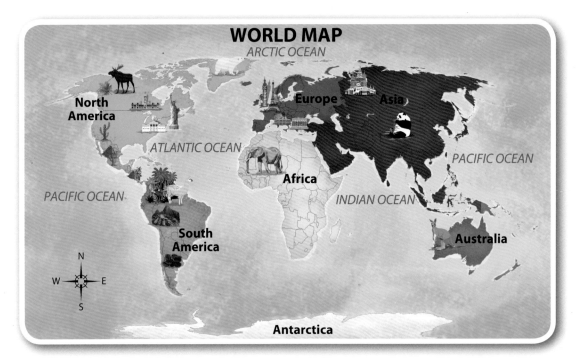

No matter what kind of map you are looking at, you need to know where north, south, east, and west are. Maps have something called a compass rose on them. A compass rose points to north, south, east

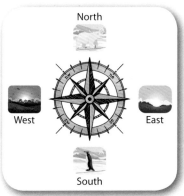

and west—the four main directions. Can you see a compass rose on the map of the world?

Maps also have symbols that stand for special places and things. For example, dots often show where cities are on a map. A star generally shows a capital city. Tiny pictures may show things such as airports, campgrounds, forests, and railroads. Triangles often show mountains, and wavy lines show rivers. Highways are shown too. Most maps have a key that explains what the symbols on a map mean.

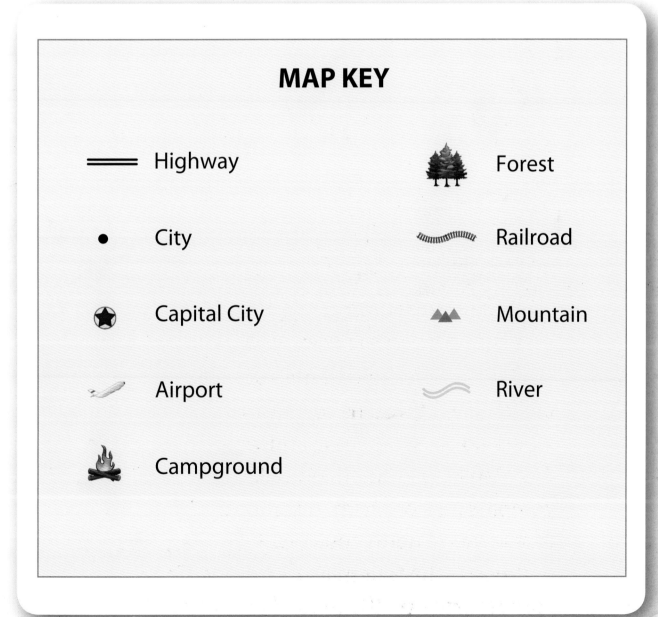

MAP KEY

═══	Highway	🌲	Forest
•	City	∿∿	Railroad
★	Capital City	▲▲	Mountain
✈	Airport	∿	River
🔥	Campground		

The United States and Canada

Almost all of the United States, Canada, Mexico, and the countries of Central America are on the continent of North America. Imagine you are taking a road trip with your family across part of North America. You are going to travel from Topeka, Kansas, where you live, all the way to Ottawa, the capital of Canada. To get to Canada, you will drive east across the United States. On your journey, you will drive through Missouri, and you will cross the mighty Mississippi River—the second longest river in the United States. You set off just as the sun is rising in the sky!

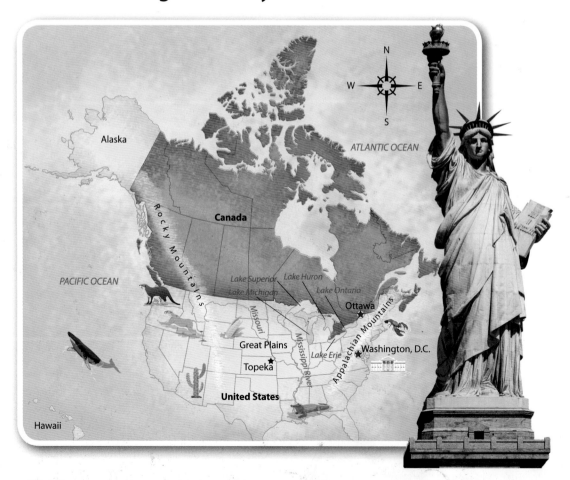

Later in the morning you reach the Mississippi River. You spot tugboats pushing large barges up and down the wide river. Your mom explains that the barges carry goods, such as grain from the Great Plains, as well as oil and coal from other parts of the United States. The barges stop at ports, or places, where these valuable things can be transported by road or by sea.

There are fifty U.S. states. You cannot visit all of them, but your road trip does take you through Indiana and Kentucky and into West Virginia. As you arrive in West Virginia, you see beautiful, mist-covered Appalachian Mountains on the horizon. You realize now why West Virginia is called the Mountain State! At almost five thousand feet, Spruce Knob is the highest mountain in West Virginia. And as well as having mountains, more than half of West Virginia is covered by forests.

You and your family have been driving for more than three days. Your journey now takes you north through the states of Ohio and Pennsylvania. By the evening you have arrived on the shore of an enormous lake called Lake Erie. You hear the waves crashing, and you see the sparkling water. On the other side of the lake is Canada. Your parents tell you that early the next day, you will be in another country!

Lake Erie is one of the Great Lakes. Altogether there are five Great Lakes. They are Lake Superior, Lake Michigan, Lake Huron, Lake Erie, and Lake Ontario.

The next day, you cross the border and arrive in Canada. Canada is the world's second-largest country. Only Russia is bigger. You have been reading about Canada on the journey and have discovered that it is divided into areas called provinces and territories. There are ten provinces, each with its own capital, and three territories.

Ottawa is the capital of Canada—and the place you are traveling to.

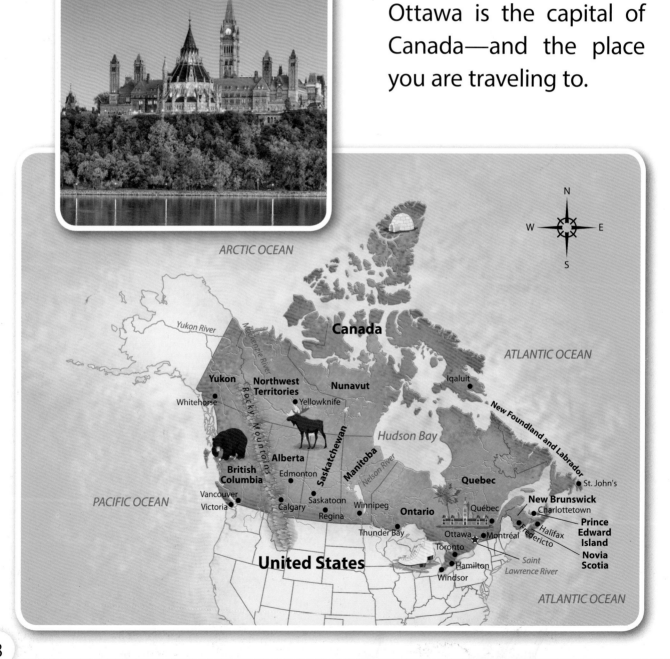

You have also discovered that fewer people live in Canada than in the United States. That's because the northern parts of Canada are very cold in the winter. Most Canadians live in the  south, near the U.S. border. But some Native Canadians, called the Inuit, do live in the far north in the territory of Nunavut, in the Canadian Arctic. Native Canadians know how to hunt and fish there. They travel across the snow on snowmobiles or sleds that are pulled by dogs.

Like the United States, Canada stretches all the way from the Atlantic Ocean to the Pacific Ocean. On the western coast of Canada is the province of British Columbia.

The Rocky Mountains run through the eastern part of the province. These are the same Rockies that run through the western United States.

Canada has open grasslands, or prairies, in parts of the south. There, herds of roaming buffalo (bison) and antelope can be found.

The northwestern part of Canada is divided into three territories. These are the Yukon Territory, the Northwest Territories, and Nunavut. The Yukon Territory is named for the Yukon River, which flows through Canada and Alaska. The Yukon River is the third longest river in North America.

In Canada, there are two official languages—English and French. That's because people who came from the countries of England and France settled there long ago. Most people who live in the Canadian province of Quebec speak French as their first language.

Canada has different money from that of the United States. For example, the British queen appears on the twenty-dollar Canadian note and the one-dollar coin. On the other side of the one-dollar coin is an image of a bird called a loon. Canadians call the one-dollar coin a loonie!

After many, many hours of traveling you finally arrive in Ottawa. It is late into the night as you drive through Parliament Hill, where the parliament buildings are lit brightly beneath the night sky. The Canadian Parliament is the seat of government in Canada, just as the U.S. Capitol in Washington, D.C., is the home of the U.S. Congress. It has been an incredible road trip, and you have learned many interesting facts about the United States and Canada. You can't wait for your next adventure!

Mexico

Mexico is on the southern border of the United States. Mexico has the world's largest population of Spanish speakers. There are thirty-one states in Mexico. Most people live in central Mexico. The northern part of Mexico is drier than the south. Because it is dry in the north, farmers use irrigation to bring water to their crops.

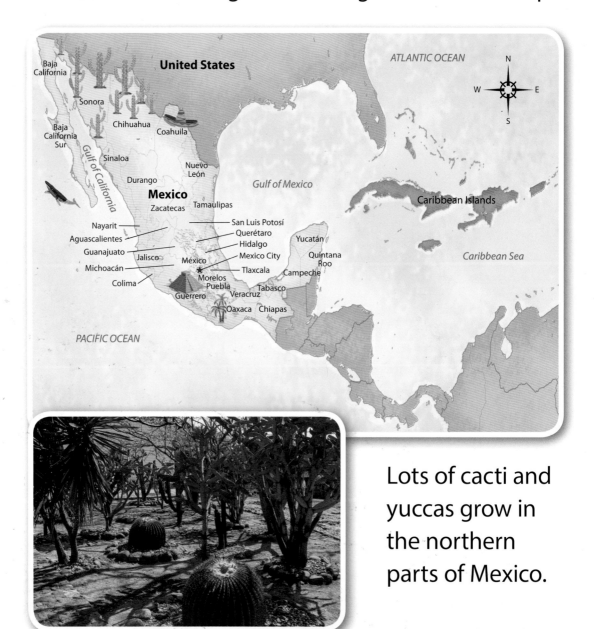

Lots of cacti and yuccas grow in the northern parts of Mexico.

Five hundred years ago, much of Mexico was ruled by the Aztec and their emperor, Moctezuma II. If Moctezuma were still alive today, he might not recognize Mexico.

Many things have changed since Moctezuma was in charge. His capital, Tenochtitlán, was the biggest city in the Americas, with thousands of people living there.

In 1519, Spanish soldiers led by Hernán Cortés conquered Moctezuma and destroyed his city. On top of the ruined city, the Spanish built an even bigger one. They called it Mexico City.

Mexico City doesn't look much like Moctezuma's capital city, but some of the ruins of the Aztec city do remain. Mexico City is the capital of Mexico today. The Spanish colonized not only Mexico, but much of Central and South America. This is why Spanish is spoken in this part of the world.

Would Moctezuma recognize anything if he traveled beyond Mexico City and through the land he once ruled over? Well, he would recognize the landscape, as much of the land is plateau surrounded

by mountains. He would also recognize the corn, called maize, and the beans, squash, and fruits that grow in the rich soil. This soil is mixed with the ash that comes from Mexico's ancient volcanoes.

What would Moctezuma think of the Mexican factories that make cars, machinery, metals, clothing, and other goods? Mexico is also a major producer of oil that is sold and transported all over the world. Moctezuma wouldn't recognize these things, but he would be happy that Mexico is a strong and successful country.

Central America

To the south of Mexico is Central America, a mountainous area of land that connects North America and South America. There are seven small countries in Central America. Can you find Guatemala on the map? Guatemala is a mountainous country with three active volcanoes. Guatemala has rainforests and is home to Lake Atitlán, the deepest lake in Central America.

CENTRAL AMERICA

N
W · E
S

Belize

Guatemala

Honduras

Lake Atitlán

El Salvador

Nicaragua

Caribbean Sea

PACIFIC OCEAN

Costa Rica

Panama

On its southern end, Lake Atitlán is surrounded by three volcanoes.

Although conquered by the Spanish, many of the people in Guatemala are descendants of the Maya people. The Maya of Guatemala built a mighty empire with great cities and tall pyramids

hundreds of years before the Aztec built their empire in Mexico.

Maya farmers grew maize and beans, as do the farmers of today. But today's Guatemalan farmers are known for their delicious coffee beans and bananas. They also produce sugar. They sell these products to countries around the world.

The country of Belize is east of Guatemala. Much of this country is covered with a thick rainforest full of wildlife. Bananas and citrus fruits are important crops in this country.

The country of Honduras is the second largest country in Central America. Like its neighbor, Guatemala, it has high mountains, rainforests, and low coastal lands. It is the only country in Central America that does not have volcanoes. Scientists travel to Honduras to learn about the plants and animals in the cloud forests.

Next to the western part of Honduras, on the Pacific, is El Salvador. El Salvador is the smallest country in Central America. This tiny country is known as the Land of the Volcanoes because about twenty of them are active. The ash from the volcanoes is good for farmers' corn, rice, and bean crops, as it improves the soil.

Nicaragua is roughly the size of New York State. It is the largest country in Central America. It too has active volcanoes and is often shaken by earthquakes. Because it's a land of strong winds, hot sun, and active volcanoes, its people use these natural resources. These wind turbines are used to create electricity.

The country of Costa Rica is south of Nicaragua and north of Panama. Costa Rica has two major mountain ranges, as well as active volcanoes. Tourism is important to Costa Rica. People from all over the world go there to enjoy the beautiful beaches and to zip line through the cloud forests.

The southernmost country in Central America is Panama. Panama is a narrow strip of land. It is the home of a canal that connects the Atlantic Ocean to the Pacific Ocean. Before the canal was built, ships carrying goods sailed all the way around the southern tip of South America to get from one ocean to the other. This was a long and dangerous journey. Today, thousands of ships pass through the canal, which has been expanded to carry even more traffic.

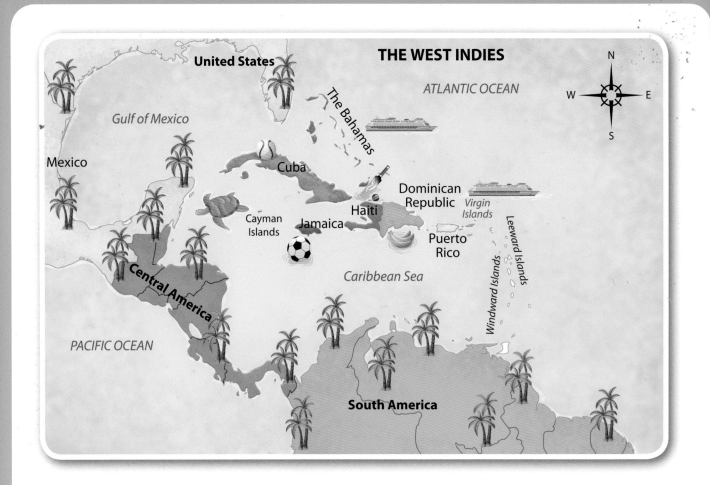

THE WEST INDIES

In the waters off the southern tip of the United States, stretching all the way down to the northern coast of South America, are a group of beautiful islands called the West Indies. Many of the islands

are in the Caribbean Sea. One of these islands, Puerto Rico, is part of the United States. However, Puerto Rico is not a state but is instead a self-governing territory. The capital of Puerto Rico is San Juan. Cuba is the largest of all the islands in the West Indies. The U.S. Virgin Islands are also in the Caribbean Sea.

CHAPTER 5

South America

There are twelve countries on the continent of South America. But more than half of South America's population lives on the larger, eastern side of this continent, in the country of Brazil. In fact, Brazil is the largest country in South America. Brazil is just a little bit

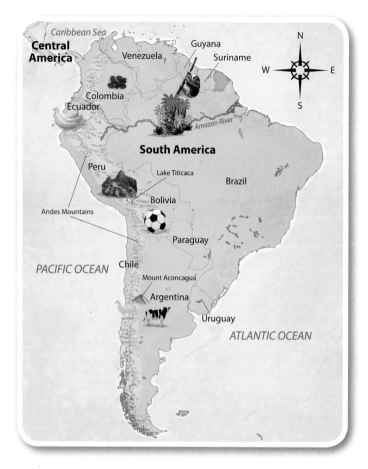

smaller than the United States. As you have discovered, long ago a lot of South America was colonized by Spain. Today, many people there speak Spanish. However, people in Brazil speak Portuguese because people from Portugal settled there. This sign on a beach in Brazil says "danger" in Portuguese.

The Andes Mountain range is in South America. The highest mountain in the Western Hemisphere is Aconcagua, which is in the southern Andes, in the country of Argentina. The highest and largest

lake in South America is Lake Titicaca, which sits in two countries—Bolivia and Peru. And the second longest river in the world, the Amazon River, is on this continent too.

Much of the world's largest tropical rainforest is in Brazil. It is called the Amazon Rainforest because the Amazon River winds its way through the hot, steamy forest. The Amazon Rainforest is home to millions of different kinds of plants and animals that you can't find anywhere else in the world.

Large areas of the rainforest have been cut down so that the lumber, or wood, can be sold. The rainforest is also being cleared so that the land can be used for farming, ranching, and other things.

Scientists worry that if too much of the rainforest is cut down, the plants and animals in it will die. One incredible creature found there is the completely see-through glass frog. Also, many of the rainforest plants, such as Cinchona, or quinine bark, are used in modern medicine.

On the north coast of South America are the two countries of Colombia and Venezuela. Northern Colombia sits on the Caribbean Sea, and western Colombia is on the Pacific Ocean. Colombia is famous for its delicious coffee.

Venezuela is on the northern coast of South America. Venezuela has two seasons—a rainy season and a dry season. Venezuela, along with other South American countries, fought Spain for its freedom. In the early 1800s, a Venezuelan named Simón Bolívar helped lead the fight. Thanks to him, in 1821, Colombia and Venezuela won their independence.

Large parts of the South American countries of Peru, Ecuador, and Bolivia are very high up in the Andes Mountains. More than half of the people in these three countries are indigenous people who have lived there for a very long time. The equator—an imaginary line halfway between the North and the South Poles—runs right through Ecuador. In fact, *ecuador* is the Spanish word for equator!

You probably think that Ecuador is very hot, since it is on the equator. Well, you are partly right. Part of Ecuador is on the Pacific coast, and there it is hot and wet. But you can actually find snow right on the equator, in Ecuador. The mountain peaks are so high and the air is so cold that the snow there never melts.

Because it is hot and wet along the coast, it is a good place to grow bananas. Ecuador grows and sells more bananas than any other country in South America. And Ecuador is one of the world's largest growers of cacao, the main ingredient for chocolate.

Peru, like Ecuador, has a coast on the Pacific Ocean. Part of the Andes Mountain range is also in Peru. The mighty Amazon River begins in Peru. Ships from the Atlantic Ocean travel more than two thousand miles up the Amazon River to the Peruvian city of Iquitos. This means Peru can transport goods across the Pacific Ocean and the Atlantic Ocean.

Like Ecuador and Peru, a large part of the South American country of Bolivia is high up in the Andes Mountains. Most people in Bolivia live in the mountains. Bolivia has more indigenous people than any other country in South America. As you have discovered, part of Lake Titicaca, the highest navigable lake in the world, is in Bolivia. The largest salt flats in the world are there also.

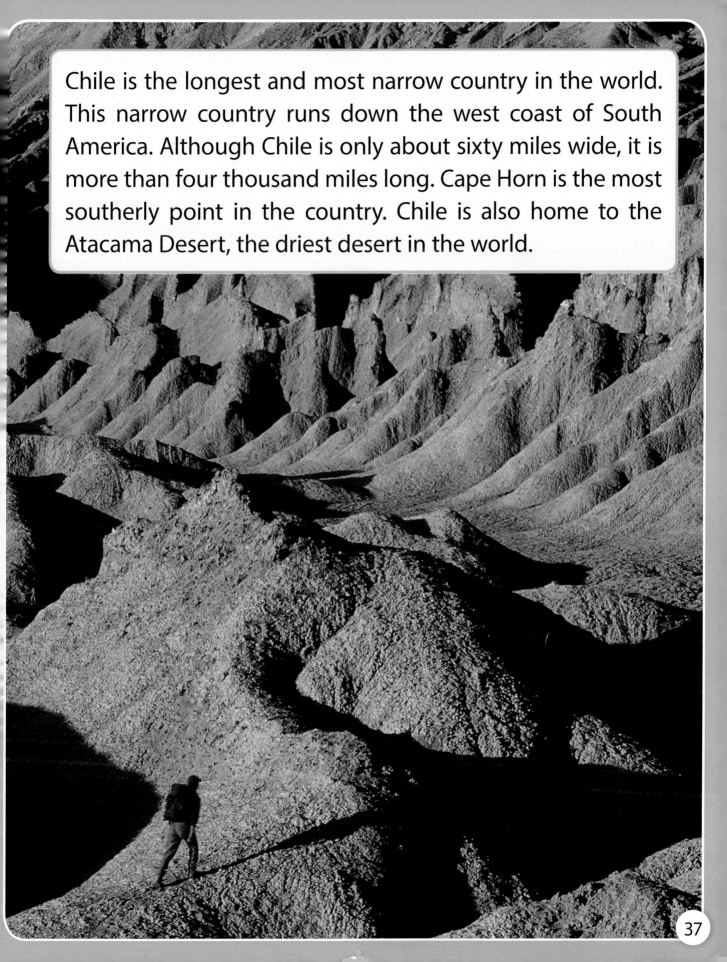

Chile is the longest and most narrow country in the world. This narrow country runs down the west coast of South America. Although Chile is only about sixty miles wide, it is more than four thousand miles long. Cape Horn is the most southerly point in the country. Chile is also home to the Atacama Desert, the driest desert in the world.

East of Chile are the countries of Argentina, Paraguay, and Uruguay. There is an area of large, flat, plains where grasses grow that spreads from Argentina to Uruguay. These plains are called the Pampas. The Pampas is very much like the Great Plains in the United States, where wheat grows and cattle graze. In fact, cowboys called gauchos still herd cattle on the Pampas.

Paraguay is one of the world's top producers of soybeans. Soybeans are an important crop used to feed farm animals, and are also used in many of the foods we eat.

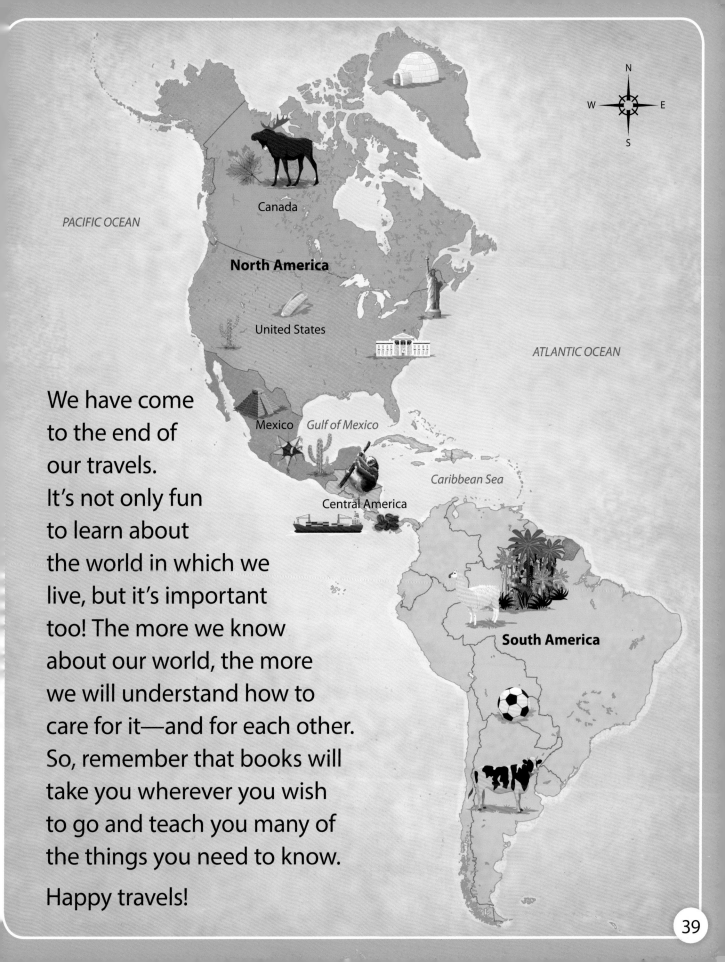

PACIFIC OCEAN

Canada

North America

United States

ATLANTIC OCEAN

Mexico   *Gulf of Mexico*

Caribbean Sea

Central America

We have come
to the end of
our travels.
It's not only fun
to learn about
the world in which we
live, but it's important
too! The more we know
about our world, the more
we will understand how to
care for it—and for each other.
So, remember that books will
take you wherever you wish
to go and teach you many of
the things you need to know.

Happy travels!

South America

Core Knowledge®

CKHG™
Core Knowledge HISTORY AND GEOGRAPHY™

Series Editor-in-Chief
E. D. Hirsch Jr.

Editorial Directors
Linda Bevilacqua and Rosie McCormick

Subject Matter Expert

Charles F. Gritzner, PhD

Distinguished Professor Emeritus of Geography, South Dakota State University

Illustration and Photo Credits